DEAR DARK FACES:

Portraits of a People

Selected and Illustrated by
Helen Earle Simcox

LOTUS PRESS
Detroit
1980

Copyright © 1980
By Helen Earle Simcox

First Edition
First Printing

All rights reserved

LC: 79-92240
ISBN: 0-916418-23-5

Printed in the United States of America

MEMBER
COSMEP
COMMITTEE OF SMALL MAGAZINE
EDITORS AND PUBLISHERS
BOX 703 SAN FRANCISCO. CA. 94101

Lotus Press, Inc.
Post Office Box 21607
Detroit, Michigan 48221

*To the "world-wide dusk of dear dark faces"
to whom Langston Hughes' life and art
were dedicated*

ACKNOWLEDGMENTS

The editor is grateful to the following poets, their representatives, and their publishers for permission to reprint copyrighted material:

LEWIS ALEXANDER: "Negro Woman" from *Caroling Dusk,* ed. Countee Cullen. Copyright 1927 by Harper & Row, Publishers, Inc.; renewed 1955 by Ida M. Cullen. Reprinted by permission of Harper & Row, Publishers, Inc.

HOUSTON A. BAKER, JR.: "Black Woman," "For Billy and Helen's Second," and "Return to My Parents' Home, Christmas, 1979" from *No Matter Where You Travel, You Still Be Black* by Houston A. Baker, Jr. Copyright 1979 by Houston A. Baker, Jr. Reprinted by permission of the author.

GWENDOLYN B. BENNETT: "To a Dark Girl" from *Caroling Dusk,* ed. Countee Cullen. Copyright 1927 by Harper & Row, Publishers, Inc.; renewed 1955 by Ida M. Cullen. Reprinted by permission of Harper & Row, Publishers, Inc.

LEBERT BETHUNE: "Harlem Freeze Frame" reprinted by permission of the author.

JILL WITHERSPOON BOYER: "But I Say" from *Dream Farmer* by Jill Witherspoon Boyer. Copyright 1975 by Jill Witherspoon Boyer. Reprinted by permission of the author.

GWENDOLYN BROOKS: "Weaponed Woman" from *Selected Poems* by Gwendolyn Brooks. Copyright 1963 by Gwendolyn Brooks Blakely. Reprinted by permission of Harper & Row, Publishers, Inc.

JONATHAN HENDERSON BROOKS: "Muse in Late November" from *The Resurrection and Other Poems* by Jonathan Henderson Brooks, copyright 1948 by The Kaleidograph Press.

STERLING A. BROWN: "Chillen Get Shoes," "Maumee Ruth," and "When de Saints Go Ma'ching Home" from *Southern Road* (Harcourt, Brace, 1932; reprinted by Beacon Press, 1974). Copyright by Sterling A. Brown. Reprinted by permission of the author.

LUCILLE CLIFTON: "My Mama Moved Among the Days" from *Good Times* by Lucille Clifton, Random House, 1969. Reprinted by permission of the author.

COUNTEE CULLEN: "Uncle Jim" from *Copper Sun* by Countee Cullen. Copyright 1925 by Harper & Row, Publishers, Inc.; renewed 1953 by Ida M. Cullen. Reprinted by permission of Harper & Row, Publishers, Inc.

MARGARET DANNER: "Passive Resistance" reprinted by permission of Margaret Esse Danner.

GLORIA DAVIS: "To Egypt" from *The New Black Poetry,* ed. Clarence Major, copyright 1969. Reprinted by permission of International Publishers Company, Inc.

TOI DERRICOTTE: "The Funeral Parade" from *The Empress of the Death House* by Toi Derricotte, copyright 1978 by Toi Derricotte; reprinted by permission of the author.

OWEN DODSON: "Black Mother Praying" and "Poems for My Brother Kenneth (IV, IX)" from *Powerful Long Ladder* by Owen Dodson, published by Farrar, Straus & Giroux. Reprinted by permission of the author.

JAMES A. EMANUEL: "Black Muslim Boy in the Hospital," copyright by James A. Emanuel. Reprinted by permission of the author.

MARI EVANS: "And the Old Women Gathered" and "The Rebel" from *I Am a Black Woman* published by Wm. Morrow Company, 1970; reprinted by permission of the author.

NAOMI FAUST: "Danny Rides the Bus," copyright by Naomi Faust. Reprinted by permission of the author.

DONALD D. GOVAN: "Recollection" from *The New Black Poetry* edited by Clarence Major, copyright 1969. Reprinted by permission of International Publishers Company, Inc.

DONALD GREEN: "Growing Clean," "Poem for a Certain Black Woman," and "Telegram to One Rotten Stepmother," copyright Donald Green. Reprinted by permission of the author.

ANGELINA WELD GRIMKÉ: "I Weep" from *Caroling Dusk*, ed. Countee Cullen. Copyright 1927 by Harper & Row, Publishers, Inc.; renewed 1955 by Ida M. Cullen. Reprinted by permission of Harper & Row, Publishers, Inc.

ROBERT HAYDEN: "The Whipping" and "Those Winter Sundays" from *Angle of Ascent, New and Selected Poems,* by Robert Hayden. Copyright © 1975, 1972, 1970, 1966 by Robert Hayden. Reprinted by permission of Liveright Publishing Corporation. "Obituary" reprinted by permission of the author.

LANGSTON HUGHES: "Poem to a Black Beloved," "Troubled Woman," and "When Sue Wears Red" from *Selected Poems of Langston Hughes* by Langston Hughes. Copyright 1926 by Alfred A. Knopf, Inc.; renewed 1954 by Langston Hughes. Reprinted by permission of Alfred A. Knopf, Inc.

LANCE JEFFERS: "An Aspect of Myself," "Depth," "In My Jugular," and "Trellie: I Am Full of Her" from *O Africa, Where I Baked My Bread* by Lance Jeffers, copyright 1977 by Lance Jeffers; reprinted by permission of the author. "Black Soul of the Land" and "Breath in My Nostrils" from *My Blackness Is the Beauty of This Land* and *When I Know the Power of My Black Hand* by Lance Jeffers; reprinted by permission of the author.

GEORGIA DOUGLAS JOHNSON: "Little Son" and "Old Black Men" from *Caroling Dusk,* ed. Countee Cullen. Copyright 1927 by Harper & Row, Publishers, Inc.; renewed 1955 by Ida M. Cullen. Reprinted by permission of Harper & Row, Publishers, Inc.

JAMES WELDON JOHNSON: "The Black Mammy" from *St. Peter Relates an Incident* by James Weldon Johnson, copyright © 1963 by Grace Nail Johnson. All rights reserved. Reprinted by permission of Viking Penguin, Inc.

ETHERIDGE KNIGHT: "He Sees Through Stone," "It Was a Funky Deal," and "To Dinah Washington" from *Poems from Prison* by Etheridge Knight, published by Broadside Press. Copyright 1968 by Etheridge Knight. Reprinted by permission of the author.

PEARL CLEAGE LOMAX: "Mississippi Born," copyright 1978 by Pearl Cleage Lomax; "Retrospect," copyright 1979 by Pearl Cleage Lomax. Reprinted by permission of the author.

AUDRE LORDE: "Black Mother Woman" and "Naturally," copyright Audre Lorde. Reprinted by permission of the author.

NAOMI LONG MADGETT: "Nocturne" and "Tree of Heaven" from *Star by Star* by Naomi Long Madgett. Copyright 1965, 1970 by Naomi Long Madgett. "Offspring" from *Pink Ladies in the Afternoon* by Naomi Long Madgett. Copyright 1972 by Naomi Long Madgett. "Lost Song" from *Exits and Entrances* by Naomi Long Madgett. Copyright 1978, Naomi Long Madgett. "Twice a Child," copyright 1978 by Naomi Long Madgett. Reprinted by permission of the author.

MADHUBUTI, HAKI (DON L. LEE): "Big Momma" and "Judy One" from *We Walk the Way of the New World* by Haki R. Madhubuti (Don L. Lee) published by Broadside Press, Detroit, Michigan. Reprinted by permission of the author.

CLAUDE McKAY: "December, 1919" and "The White House" from *Selected Poems of Claude McKay,* copyright 1953 by Twayne Publishers, Inc.; reprinted by permission of Twayne Publishers, A Division of G. K. Hall & Co.

MAY MILLER: "Child in the Night," "The Scream," and "Three Scenes for All Men" from *Dust of Uncertain Journey* by May Miller. Copyright 1975 by May Miller. Reprinted by permission of the author.

GABRIEL OKARA: "Once Upon a Time" from *Poems From Black Africa,* ed. Langston Hughes. Copyright © 1963 by Langston Hughes. Reprinted by permission of Indiana University Press.

DUDLEY RANDALL: "The Rite" from *Cities Burning* by Dudley Randall. Copyright 1968 by Dudley Randall. Reprinted by permission of the author. "Blackberry Sweet," copyright by Dudley Randall. Reprinted by permission of the author.

EDWARD S. SPRIGGS: "my beige mom" from *Black Dialogue Magazine.* Copyright 1967 by *Black Dialogue Magazine.* Reprinted by permission of the author and Black Dialogue.

JEAN TOOMER: "Face" and "Calling Jesus" from *Cane* by Jean Toomer. Copyright 1923 by Boni & Liveright; renewed 1951 by Jean Toomer. Reprinted by permission of Liveright Publishing Corporation.

PAULETTE CHILDRESS WHITE: "Big Maybelle," "Humbled Rocks," "Oronde," and "Say That I Am" from *Love Poem to a Black Junkie* by Paulette C. White, copyright 1975 by Paulette Childress White. Reprinted by permission of the author.

CONTENTS

One: MOTHERS

    Oronde *(Paulette Childress White)*   15
    My Mama Moved Among the Days *(Lucille Clifton)*   16
    Recollection *(Donald D. Govan)*   17
    My Beige Mom *(Edward S. Spriggs)*   18
    Black Mother Woman *(Audre Lorde)*   19
    Big Momma *(Haki Madhubuti)*   20
    Black Woman *(Georgia Douglas Johnson)*   22
    When de Saints Go Ma'ching Home (V)
        (Sterling A. Brown)   23
    Maumee Ruth *(Sterling A. Brown)*   24
    Mississippi Born *(Pearl Cleage Lomax)*   25
    The Black Mammy *(James Weldon Johnson)*   26

Two: THOSE WHO WEEP

    I Weep *(Angelina Weld Grimké)*   29
    Troubled Woman *(Langston Hughes)*   30
    Face *(Jean Toomer)*   31
    Calling Jesus *(Jean Toomer)*   32
    The Scream *(May Miller)*   33
    December, 1919 *(Claude McKay)*   34
    Lost Song *(Naomi Long Madgett)*   35
    Poems for My Brother Kenneth (IV, IX) *(Owen Dodson)*   36
    Depth *(Lance Jeffers)*   38
    Negro Woman *(Lewis Alexander)*   39
    The Whipping *(Robert Hayden)*   40
    Black Muslim Boy in a Hospital *(James A. Emanuel)*   41
    The Funeral Parade *(Toi Derricotte)*   42

Three: THE GENERATIONS

    Old Black Men *(Georgia Douglas Johnson)*   45
    Little Son *(Georgia Douglas Johnson)*   46
    And the Old Women Gathered *(Mari Evans)*   47
    Once Upon a Time *(Gabriel Okara)*   48
    The Rite *(Dudley Randall)*   50
    Muse in Late November *(Jonathan Henderson Brooks)*   51
    Chillen Get Shoes *(Sterling A. Brown)*   52
    Offspring *(Naomi Long Madgett)*   53
    Twice a Child *(Naomi Long Madgett)*   54
    Those Winter Sundays *(Robert Hayden)*   55
    An Aspect of Myself *(Lance Jeffers)*   56
    Return to My Parents' Home, Christmas, 1979
        (Houston A. Baker, Jr.)   57
    Retrospect *(Pearl Cleage Lomax)*   58

Four: SHEBA'S DAUGHTERS

To a Dark Girl *(Gwendolyn B. Bennett)*   61
Judy-One *(Haki Madhubuti)*   62
Naturally *(Audre Lorde)*   63
Poem: To the Black Beloved *(Langston Hughes)*   64
When Sue Wears Red *(Langston Hughes)*   65
To Dinah Washington *(Etheridge Knight)*   66
Nocturne *(Naomi Long Madgett)*   67
Say That I Am *(Paulette Childress White)*   68
Blackberry Sweet *(Dudley Randall)*   69
Black Woman *(Houston A. Baker, Jr.)*   70
To Egypt *(Gloria Davis)*   71
Trellie: I Am Full of Her *(Lance Jeffers)*   72

Five: REBELS

Growing Clean *(Donald Green)*   75
Telegram to One Rotten Stepmother *(Donald Green)*   76
Poem for a Certain Black Woman *(Donald Green)*   77
Harlem Freeze Frame *(Lebert Bethune)*   78
In My Jugular *(Lance Jeffers)*   79
Black Soul of the Land *(Lance Jeffers)*   80
Breath in My Nostrils *(Lance Jeffers)*   81
The White House *(Claude McKay)*   82
It Was a Funky Deal *(Etheridge Knight)*   83
He Sees Through Stone *(Etheridge Knight)*   84
Tree of Heaven *(Naomi Long Madgett)*   85
Uncle Jim *(Countee Cullen)*   86
The Rebel *(Mari Evans)*   87
Weaponed Woman *(Gwendolyn Brooks)*   88

Six: BLACK LAMPS

Black Mother Praying *(Owen Dodson)*   91
Passive Resistance *(Margaret Danner)*   95
Child in the Night *(May Miller)*   96
Three Scenes for All Men *(May Miller)*   97
Humbled Rocks *(Paulette Childress White)*   98
Big Maybelle *(Paulette Childress White)*   99
Obituary *(Robert Hayden)*   100
But I Say *(Jill Witherspoon Boyer)*   101
Danny Takes the Bus *(Naomi Faust)*   102
For Billy and Helen's Second *(Houston A. Baker, Jr.)*   104

Author Index

One:
MOTHERS

ORONDE

Paulette Childress White

The tangles on my baby's head
are curious
and beautiful.
His eyes
are circles of sweet mischief.
My hand of gentle Motherlove
smooths a curve of tender cheek
and the smile he gives
is truer than words
he will someday speak.

Golden sun rains down on us
and I will always remember
this moment,
richly painted on the fabric
of my clinging thought,
as even now he struggles
to free himself,
to run away
from me.

MY MAMA MOVED AMONG THE DAYS

Lucille Clifton

My Mama moved among the days
like a dreamwalker in a field;
seemed like what she touched was hers
seemed like what touched her couldn't hold,
she got us almost through the high grass
then seemed like she turned around and ran
right back in
right back on in

RECOLLECTION

Donald D. Govan

Mother was a wolf; snarled her long
Teeth at bad men who bothered us.
Mother went out at night when her
Friend the moon shone her the prickly
Path of thorns to find that which
Fed us.
I saw Mother weep within those eyes of
Cow, she'd look at me and my brother
And her fear would jump like a rabbit
From her eye into ours.
I looked at the dark woman and marveled
At the infinity of her eye painted with
The image of a black man from Texas; there
It was hot when he walked toward the
Sun. Wondering... Wondering...
Lonesome along her beings promonotory; she'd
Smile to her secret lover the moon.
She growled fierce when the fish face man
Smiled money. We: My brother and I thought yum
His juicy bone; but Mother Wolf said we were
Human. The fish face man grew as we grew.
The larger we became the more oppressive
He is. Mother Wolf wouldn't let us eat
The fish face man. We should have, but Mother
Wolf said we are human.

MY BEIGE MOM

Edward S. Spriggs

is
georgia grown
georgia bruised
tall
strong-boned
beige beauty
was
afroamerican
in the twenties
turned "negro"
in the forties
proud "american"
in the sixties
will
die a christian
in california
tall, strong-boned
beige & bruised
i
took her strength
in thirty-four
now with love i
lay it at the
third world's door

BLACK MOTHER WOMAN

Audre Lorde

I cannot recall you gentle.
Through your heavy love
I have become
an image of your once delicate flesh
split with deceitful longings.
When strangers come and compliment me
your aged spirit takes a bow
jingling with pride
but once you hid that secret
in the center of furies
hanging me
with deep breasts and wiry hair
with your own split flesh and long suffering eyes
buried in myths of no worth.

But I have peeled away your anger
down to its core of love
and look mother
I am
a dark temple where your true spirit rises
beautiful and tough as a chestnut
stanchion against your nightmares of weakness
and if my eyes conceal
a squadron of conflicting rebellions
I learned from you
to define myself
through your denials.

BIG MOMMA

Haki Madhubuti
(Don L. Lee)

finally retired   pensionless
from cleaning somebody else's house
she remained home to clean
the one she didn't own.

in her kitchen where we often talked
the *chicago tribune* served as a tablecloth
for the two cups of tomato soup that went
along with my weekly visit & talkingto.

she was in a seriously-funny mood
& from the get-go she was down, realdown:

>roaches around here are like
>letters on a newspaper
>or
>u gonta be a writer, hunh
>when u gone write me some writen
>or
>the way niggers act around here
>if talk cd kill we'd all be dead.

she's somewhat confused about all this *blackness*
but said that it's good when negroes start putting themselves
first and added: we've always shopped at the colored stores,
>   & the way niggers cut each other up round
>   here every weekend that whiteman don't
>   haveta
>   worry bout no revolution specially when he's
>   gonta haveta pay for it too, anyhow all he's
>   gotta do is drop a truck load of *dope* out
>   there
>   on 43rd st. & all the niggers & yr
>   revolutionaries
>   be too busy getten high & then they'll turn
>   round
>   and fight each other over who got the
>   mostest.

We finished our soup and i moved to excuse myself,
as we walked to the front door she made a last comment:

      now *luther* i knows you done changed a lots but if
      you can think back, we never did eat too much pork
      round here anyways, it was bad for the belly.
i shared her smile and agreed.

touching the snow lightly i headed for 43rd st.
at the corner i saw a brother crying   while
trying to hold up a lamp post,
thru his watery eyes i cd see big momma's words.

at sixty-eight
she moves freely, is often right
and when there is food
eats   joyously with her own
real teeth.

BLACK WOMAN

Georgia Douglas Johnson

Don't knock at my door, little child,
   I cannot let you in,
You know not what a world this is
   Of cruelty and sin.
Wait in the still eternity
   Until I come to you,
The world is cruel, cruel, child,
   I cannot let you in!

Don't knock at my door, little one,
   I cannot bear the pain
Of turning deaf-ear to your call
   Time and time again!
You do not know the monster men
   Inhabiting the earth,
Be still, be still, my precious child,
   I must not give you birth!

From WHEN DE SAINTS GO MA'CHING HOME

Sterling A. Brown

5.

Ise got a dear ole mudder
She is in hebben I know —
He sees:
    Mammy,
    Li'l mammy — wrinkled face,
    Her brown eyes quick to tears — to joy —
    With such happy pride in her
    Guitar-plunkin' boy.
    Oh kain't I be one in nummer?

    Mammy
    With deep religion defeating the grief
    Life piled so closely about her,
    Ise so glad trouble doan last alway,
    And her dogged belief
    That some fine day
    She'd go a-ma'chin'
    When de saints go ma'chin' home.

He sees her ma'chin' home, ma'chin' along,
Her perky joy shining in her furrowed face,
Her weak and quavering voice singing her song —
The best chair set apart for her worn out body
In that restful place . . . .
    I pray to de Lawd I'll meet her
    When de saints go ma'chin' home.

MAUMEE RUTH
Sterling A. Brown

Might as well bury her
    And bury her deep,
Might as well put her
    Where she can sleep.

Might as well lay her
    Out in her shiny black;
And for the love of God
    Not wish her back.

Maum Sal may miss her
    Maum Sal, she only
With no one now to scoff
    Sal may be lonely . . . .

Nobody else there is
    Who will be caring
How rocky was the road
    For her wayfaring;

Nobody be heeding in
    Cabin, or town
That she is lying here
    In her best gown.

Boy that she suckled
    How should he know
Hiding in city holes
    Sniffing the 'snow'?

And how should the news
    Pierce Harlem's din
To reach her baby gal,
    Sodden with gin?

To cut her withered heart
    They cannot come again,
Preach her the lies about
    Jordan and then

Might as well drop her
    Deep in the ground
Might as well pray for her
    That she sleep sound . . . .

MISSISSIPPI BORN
(For Ayanna Pearl Williams)

Pearl Cleage Lomax

your voice sister
tells me another child has come.
your tired voice tells more
than your words or eyes will say.
another child has come.
and the birthroom
filled with blood and small groans
and your daughter's round eyes leaning to watch
her tiny sister born.

driving the Mississippi death roads to find you.
the childfilled jeep bumps and jiggles
until I cannot tell if the riding or the fear
thrusts my heart into my throat.
emmett till fills my head like damp cotton
and chaney's neshoba nightmare is more real
on this road that slithers toward Meridian,
Jackson, Sunflower County, Braxton and D'Lo.
your house squatting in the midst of clots
of dry dirt crumbled for the futile planting.
and crouched in the dark cave of that room
you greeting me.   tired
and sick of being sick here.
wild eyes gleaming in wild face and the lump
of mewing new one curled like a sleeping slug beside you.

am i real to you now?
remember the night of your first leaving?
your long blue scarf doublewrapped against the cold
at the end of that week when we could not laugh
together without collapsing into giggles and tears
laying our watery cheeks against the cool dry bathroom porcelain
hugging each other and hugging ourselves.

are you real to me now?
swishing away the constant flies and rocking the new one.
thinking that the flies whisper of death and decay
and cannot be allowed to skitter across her tiny red face.
sister sister
another child has come.

THE BLACK MAMMY

James Weldon Johnson

O whitened head entwined in turban gay,
O kind black face, O crude, but tender hand,
O foster-mother in whose arms there lay
The race whose sons are masters of the land!
It was thine arms that sheltered in their fold,
It was thine eyes that followed through the length
Of infant days these sons. In times of old
It was thy breast that nourished them to strength.

So often hast thou to thy bosom pressed
The golden head, the face and brow of snow;
So often has it 'gainst thy broad, dark breast
Lain, set off like a quickened cameo.
Thou simple soul, as cuddling down that babe
With thy sweet croon, so plaintive and so wild,
Came ne'er the thought to thee, swift like a stab,
That it some day might crush thy own black child?

Two:
THOSE WHO WEEP

I WEEP

Angelina Weld Grimké

     — I weep —
Not as the young do noisily,
Not as the aged rustily,
    But quietly.
Drop by drop the great tears
Splash upon my hands,
And save you saw them shine,
    You would not know
      I wept.

TROUBLED WOMAN

Langston Hughes

She stands
In the quiet darkness,
This troubled woman,
Bowed by
Weariness and pain,
Like an
Autumn flower
In the frozen rain.
Like a
Wind-blown autumn flower
That never lifts its head
Again.

FACE

Jean Toomer

HAIR —
silver-gray,
like streams of stars,
Brows —
recurved canoes
quivered by the ripples blown by pain,

Her eyes —
mist of tears
condensing on the flesh below
And her channeled muscles
are cluster grapes of sorrow
purple in the evening sun
nearly ripe for worms.

CALLING JESUS

Jean Toomer

Her soul is like a little thrust-tailed dog that follows her, whimpering. She is large enough, I know, to find a warm spot for it. But each night when she comes home and closes the big outside storm door, the little dog is left in the vestibule, filled with chills till morning. Some one ... eoho Jesus ... soft as a cotton boll brushed against the milk-pod cheek of Christ, will steal in and cover it that it need not shiver, and carry it to her where she sleeps upon clean hay cut in her dreams.

When you meet her in the daytime on the streets, the little dog keeps coming. Nothing happens at first, and then, when she has forgotten the streets and alleys, and the large house where she goes to bed of nights, a soft thing like fur begins to rub your limbs, and you hear a low, scared voice, lonely, calling, and you know that a cool something nozzles moisture in your palms. Sensitive things like nostrils quiver. Her breath comes sweet as honeysuckle whose pistils bear the life of coming song. And her eyes carry to where builders find no need for vestibules, for swinging on iron hinges, storm doors.

Her soul is like a little thrust-tailed dog, that follows her, whimpering. I've seen it tagging on behind her, up streets where chestnut trees flowered, where dusty asphalt had been freshly sprinkled with clean water. Up alleys where niggers sat on low door-steps before tumbled shanties and sang and loved. At night, when she comes home, the little dog is left in the vestibule, nosing the crack beneath the big storm door, filled with chills till morning. Some one ... eoho Jesus ... soft as the bare feet of Christ moving across bales of southern cotton, will steal in and cover it that it need not shiver, and carry it to her where she sleeps: cradled in dream-fluted cane.

THE SCREAM

May Miller

I am a woman controlled.
Remember this: I never scream.
Yet I stood a form apart
Watching my other frenzied self
Beaten by words and wounds
Make in silence a mighty scream —
A scream that the wind took up
And thrust through the bars of night
Beyond all reason's final rim.

Out where the sea's last murmur dies
And the gull's cry has no sound,
Out where city voices fade,
Stilled in a lyric sleep
Where silence is its own design,
My scream hovered a ghost denied
Wanting the shape of lips.

DECEMBER, 1919

Claude McKay

Last night I heard your voice, mother,
    The words you sang to me
When I, a little barefoot boy,
    Knelt down against your knee.

And tears gushed from my heart, mother,
    And passed beyond its wall,
But though the fountain reached my throat
    The drops refused to fall.

'Tis ten years since you died, mother,
    Just ten dark years of pain,
And oh, I only wish that I
    Could weep just once again.

LOST SONG

Naomi Long Madgett

I lost a poem once.
Somehow I let it fall overboard
from a ship I was sailing.

I heard it splash, saw it ripple
like a silver fish in the moonlight
before the current carried it away.

I couldn't save it.
I couldn't even cry.

Sometimes I think I can still
hear it calling me, a frightened
helpless child lost

from the arms that would
have held it warm, wrenched
from the soul it would have healed.

Ever since, my ship has been
idling at half mast.

From POEMS FOR MY BROTHER KENNETH

Owen Dodson

IV

My chief citizen is dead
And my town at half-mast:
Even in speech,
Even in walking,
Even in seeing
The busy streets where he stood
And the room where he was host to his friends
And his enemies, where we erased the night to dawn
With conversations of what I had seen and he had seen
And done and written during the space of time we were
                                                          apart.

We will not talk again with common breath.
His voice has gone to talk to death.
There is a new language to learn
And I am learning like a truant child.
I do not understand this code, this life to death.
I will not be convinced that we must
Only talk again as dust to dust.

IX

Here is holly for you, brother, here is mistletoe,
Here is the song we sing this Christmas with the cold sparrow.

We come with Christmas in our arms on the day of the original
                                                                                                 Child,
But women in these blanket wreaths is sorrow, pared and wild.

It is almost a year now, nearing the twentieth day
Of the second month, when you died, so we will lay

Holly with berries, and hemlock washed and clean
For the earth to celebrate with us what you have been.

DEPTH

Lance Jeffers

We stood at the graveside waiting;
the minister's words floated trivially before us
    like taffeta on a vaguely windy day;
the coffin lay by the grave
and inside lay Roger —
dead at 45, worn out by anguish.

Suddenly Trellie was weeping
from her dark, immortal face,
the sound of perfect beauty
in her tears.

No one else was weeping;
she alone was weeping for his
    innumerable defeats, weeping for
    his kindness, grieving a stranger who
was grateful for acceptance.

Where is the boundary of her love
    for the beaten,
    for the rejected,
    for the infants and the aged,
    for the defiant and the embattled?
Where is the boundary of Trellie's love?

NEGRO WOMAN

Lewis Alexander

The sky hangs heavy tonight
Like the hair of a Negro woman.
The scars of the moon are curved
Like the wrinkles on the brow of a Negro woman.

The stars twinkle tonight
Like the glaze in a Negro woman's eyes,
Drinking the tears set flowing by an aging hurt
Gnawing at her heart.

The earth trembles tonight
Like the quiver of a Negro woman's eye-lids cupping
    tears.

THE WHIPPING

Robert Hayden

The old woman across the way
    is whipping the boy again
and shouting to the neighborhood
    her goodness and his wrongs.

Wildly he crashes through elephant ears,
    pleads in dusty zinnias,
while she in spite of crippling fat
    pursues and corners him.

She strikes and strikes the shrilly circling
    boy till the stick breaks
in her hand. His tears are rainy weather
    to woundlike memories:

My head gripped in bony vise
    of knees, the writhing struggle
to wrench free, the blows, the fear
    worse than blows that hateful

Words could bring, the face that I
    no longer knew or loved . . . .
Well, it is over now, it is over,
    and the boy sobs in his room.

And the woman leans muttering against
    a tree, exhausted, purged —
avenged in part for lifelong hidings
    she has had to bear.

BLACK MUSLIM BOY IN A HOSPITAL

James A. Emanuel

Are you hot there too?
(Down in the grates of you,
Banked for long burning,
Some cindered yearning,
Looked in despair,
Kindles your glare.)

Does it hurt? (Something cries
When I gently press your eyes.
A tiny light in you goes out,
Blinking in a stream of doubt,
When this white though healing hand
Trespasses and takes command.)

(Hate for friends and hate for foes
Who have not endured hate's blows
Digested with the crumbs of years.
What can stop these ancient tears
Burning in a little face
So captive in a starched embrace?)

THE FUNERAL PARADE

Toi Derricotte

Over the Ambassador Bridge —
an arc of perpetual pregnancy —

we ride
to bury the dead.

Leading the way is one
blind, deaf, dumb:

the path has been cut,
we are doing our duty.

Grandfather,
in spats.

Grandmother,
tailor-made.

& the small child, the mourner,
blind as the buried.

Three:
TWO GENERATIONS

OLD BLACK MEN

Georgia Douglas Johnson

They have dreamed as young men dream
    Of glory, love and power;
They have hoped as youth will hope
    Of life's sun-minted hour.

They have seen as others saw
    Their bubbles burst in air,
And they have learned to live it down
    As though they did not care.

LITTLE SON

Georgia Douglas Johnson

The very acme of my woe,
    The pivot of my pride,
My consolation, and my hope
    Deferred, but not denied.
The substance of my every dream,
    The riddle of my plight,
The very world epitomized
    In turmoil and delight.

...AND THE OLD WOMEN GATHERED
(The Gospel Singers)

Mari Evans

and the old women gathered
and sang His praises
standing
resolutely together
like supply sergeants who
have seen
everything
and are still
Regular Army: It
was fierce and
not melodic and
although we ran
the sound of it
stayed in our ears . . .

ONCE UPON A TIME

Gabriel Okara

Once upon a time, son
they used to laugh with their hearts
and laugh with their eyes;
but now they only laugh with their teeth,
while their ice-block-cold eyes
search behind my shadow.

There was a time indeed
they used to shake hands with their hearts;
but that's gone, son.
Now they shake hands without hearts
while their left hands search
my empty pockets.

"Feel at home," "Come again,"
they say, and when I come
again and feel
at home, once, twice,
there will be no thrice —
for then I find doors shut on me.

So I have learned many things, son,
I have learned to wear many faces
like dresses — homeface,
officeface, streetface, hostface, cock-
tailface, with all their conforming smiles
like a fixed portrait smile
And I have learned too
to laugh with only my teeth
and shake hands without my heart.
I have also learned to say, "Goodbye,"
when I mean "Goodriddance":
to say "Glad to meet you,"
without being glad; and to say "It's been
nice talking to you," after being bored.

But believe me, son
I want to be what I used to be
when I was like you. I want

to unlearn all these muting things.
Most of all, I want to relearn
how to laugh, for my laugh in the mirror
shows only my teeth like a snake's bare fangs!

So show me, son
how to laugh; show me how
I used to laugh and smile
Once upon a time when I was like you.

THE RITE

Dudley Randall

"Now you must die," the young one said,
"and all your art be overthrown."
The old one only bowed his head
as if those words had been his own.
And with no pity in his eyes
The young man acted out his part
and put him to the sacrifice
and drank his blood and ate his heart.

MUSE IN LATE NOVEMBER

Jonathan Henderson Brooks

I greet you, son, with joy and winter rue:
For you the fatted calf, the while I bind
Sackcloth against my heart for siring you
At sundown and the twilight. Child, you find
A sire sore tired of striving with the winds;
Climbing Mount Nebo with laborious breath
To view the land of promise through blurred lens,
Knowing he can not enter, feeling death.

And, as old Israel called his dozen sons
And placed his withered hands upon each head
Ere he was silent with the skeletons
In Mamre of the cold, cave-chambered dead,
So would I bless you with a dreamer's will:
The dream that baffles me, may you fulfill.

CHILLEN GET SHOES

Sterling A. Brown

Hush little Lily,
    Don't you cry;
You'll get your silver slippers
    Bye and bye.

Moll wears silver slippers
    With red heels,
And men come to see her
    In automobiles.

Lily walks wretched,
    Dragging her doll,
Worshipping stealthily
    Good-time Moll;

Envying bitterly
    Moll's fine clothes,
And her plump legs clad
    In openwork hose.

Don't worry, Lily,
    Don't you cry;
You'll be like Moll, too,
    Bye and bye.

OFFSPRING

Naomi Long Madgett

I tried to tell her:
    This way the twig is bent.
    Born of my trunk and strengthened by my roots,
    You must stretch newgrown branches
    Closer to the sun
    Than I can reach.
I wanted to say:
    Extend my self to that far atmosphere
    Only my dreams allow.

But the twig broke,
And yesterday I saw her
Walking down an unfamiliar street,
    Feet confident,
    Face slanted upward toward a threatening sky,
    And
    She was smiling
    And she was
    Her very free,
    Her very individual,
    Unpliable
    Own.

TWICE A CHILD
(For my mother at ninety)

Naomi Long Madgett

Butterflies fan fragile, filmy wings
in the darkening forest I lead her through,
holding her hand, guiding
her trembling footsteps, buttoning
her memory as I used to dress my dolls
when she was mother and I was child.
Now overhanging leaves filter fading gold
through shadow to the damp
and slippery ground beneath as she drifts
through the twilight of a fairy tale
whose characters' names she has forgotten.
And I can only guess what distant bells
she hears tolling at the top of the hill
she climbs on all fours.

THOSE WINTER SUNDAYS

Robert E. Hayden

Sundays too my father got up early
and put his clothes on in the blueblack cold,
then with cracked hands that ached
from labor in the weekday weather made
banked fires blaze. No one ever thanked him.

I'd wake and hear the cold splintering, breaking.
When the rooms were warm, he'd call,
and slowly I would rise and dress,
fearing the chronic angers of that house,

Speaking indifferently to him,
who had driven out the cold
and polished my good shoes as well.
What did I know, what did I know
of love's austere and lonely offices?

AN ASPECT OF MYSELF

Lance Jeffers

My mother was stripped of her morning breasts,
my father's intestines leaked out through the wound of his
                navel door,
my grandmother was stern as a virgin upon the gallows,
my grandfather gathered whole counties in his arm,
    flung a million seeds of healing from his hand:
my slave greatgrandfather was grim upon his hoe,
watched with eyes of hatred the livid whites,
my greatgrandmother was limp on her bed of snow,
        master stood over her as if she were a deer he had shot
        while he returned his penis to the holster at his hip . . . .

RETURN TO MY PARENTS' HOME, CHRISTMAS, 1979

Houston A. Baker, Jr.

The first hour of embrace
and careful silence, avoiding
vulnerabilities
and obvious change
you reach for the boy
you left behind,

sense his fear
when stepping from the last stair
into the third-floor night,
a room of charm and fetish
secure against the monsters of his day,
notorious boogies
and Southern Whites . . . his head falling toward
the pillow, a prayer, a sensual sleep . . .

Shadows in the jolly corner
recall the wonder of those days,
as you search the vesper of your parents' eyes
and find once more the strength
of their undiminished love.

Your son looks on, awaits his turn, as
the season begins again.

RETROSPECT

Pearl Cleage Lomax

Old woman —
I can see you
huddled in your
window
remembering now ancient
lovers
who are as withered
as you.
Wrapped tightly in
your shawl
your eyes no longer look
out
but only peer in.
The fragile gold frames
of your dusty glasses
are almost a shield
but not quite
and every once in a while
I can see you shiver
in a space between
memories.

Four:
SHEBA'S DAUGHTERS

TO A DARK GIRL

Gwendolyn B. Bennett

I love you for your brownness
And the rounded darkness of your breast.
I love you for the breaking sadness in your voice
And shadows where your wayward eye-lids rest.

Something of old forgotten queens
Lurks in the lithe abandon of your walk
And something of the shackled slave
Sobs in the rhythm of your talk.

Oh, little brown girl, born for sorrow's mate,
Keep all you have of queenliness,
Forgetting that you once were slave,
And let your full lips laugh at Fate!

JUDY-ONE

Haki Madhubuti
(Don L. Lee)

she's the camera's
subject:
the sun for colored film.

her smile is like
clear light bouncing off
the darkness of the
mediterranean at nighttime.

we all know it,
her smile.
when it's working,
moves like sea water —
always going somewhere

strongly.

NATURALLY

Audre Lorde

Since Naturally Black is Naturally Beautiful
I must be proud
And, naturally,
Black and
Beautiful
Who always was a trifle
Yellow
And plain though proud
Before.

I've given up pomades
Having spent the summer sunning
And feeling naturally free
    (if I die of skin cancer
    oh well — one less
    black and beautiful me)
Yet no agency spends millions
To prevent my summer tanning
And who trembles nightly
With the fear of their lily cities being swallowed
By a summer ocean of naturally wooly hair?

But I've bought my can of
Natural Hair Spray
Made and marketed in Watts
Still thinking more
Proud beautiful black women
Could better make and use
Black bread.

POEM: TO THE BLACK BELOVED

Langston Hughes

Ah,
My black one,
Thou art not beautiful
Yet thou hast
A loveliness
Surpassing beauty.

Oh,
My black one,
Thou art not good
Yet thou hast
A purity
Surpassing goodness.

Ah,
My black one,
Thou art not luminous
Yet an altar of jewels,
An altar of shimmering jewels,
Would pale in the light
Of thy darkness,
Pale in the light of thy nightness.

WHEN SUE WEARS RED

Langston Hughes

When Susanna Jones wears red
Her face is like an ancient cameo
Turned brown by the ages.

Come with a blast of trumpets,
    Jesus!

When Susanna Jones wears red
A queen from some time-dead Egyptian night
Walks once again.

Blow trumpets, Jesus!

And the beauty of Susanna Jones in red
Burns in my heart a love-fire sharp like pain.

Sweet silver trumpets,
    Jesus!

TO DINAH WASHINGTON

Etheridge Knight

I have heard your voice floating, royal and real,
Across the dusky neighborhoods,
And the eyes of old men grow bright, remembering;
Children stop their play to listen,
Remembering — though they have never heard you before,
You are familiar to them:
Queen of the Blues, singing an eternal song.

In the scarred booths of Forty-Third street,
"Long Johns" suck in their bellies,
On the brass-studded leather of Elite-town,
Silk-suited Bucks raise their chins . . .

Wherever a man is without a warm woman,
Or a woman without her muscled man,
The eternal song is sung.

Some say you're sleeping.
But I say you're singing.

Unforgettable Queen.

NOCTURNE

Naomi Long Madgett

See how dark the night settles on my face,
How deep the rivers of my soul
Flow imperturbable and strong.

Rhythms of unremembered jungles
Pulse through the untamed shadows of my song,
And my cry is the dusky accent of secret midnight birds.

Above the sable valleys of my sorrow
My swarthy hands have fashioned
Pyramids of virgin joy.

See how tenderly God pulls His blanket of blackness over
                              the earth.
You think I am not beautiful?
You lie!

SAY THAT I AM

Paulette Childress White

Say that I am beautiful.
Say that I am
because my face is ebony
of an African tree
and queenly Benin bronze,
yet by rift of time
and fire of slavery,
distinctly mine.

Say that I am
because my body,
bold and still strong,
blossoming sweet
with secret promises
or fulfilled and swollen
with life,
is Mother of the Earth

and my legs,
like sleek flamingoes on the Nile,
strut straight and proud
against cold Western winds;

because I love a man
and mother children
in a world that has denied me —
tried to strip me bare
and take my love away.

Say that I am
because I keep the song
and dance
the smile
eternally.

Because my soul is constant source,
Sun-giving warmth
and light
and life,

say that I am beautiful.
Say that I am!

BLACKBERRY SWEET

Dudley Randall

Black girl black girl
lips as curved as cherries
full as grape bunches
sweet as blackberries

Black girl black girl
when you walk you are
magic as a rising bird
or a falling star

Black girl black girl
what's your spell to make
the heart in my breast
jump   stop   shake

BLACK WOMAN

Houston A. Baker, Jr.

And you are lithe
Fretted
Soft beyond our stares.
Calm lady of the skies

The clouds belong to you

'Cause even when
You're not moving
You're flying.

TO EGYPT

Gloria Davis

Where are my people?
When will your tales unfurl,
            and let the white world know
you were once my mother
and I
your soft kinky headed girl . . .
Tell them —
White America, I mean,
how you built me a strong black nation
            from a vibrant black seed!
Tell them that my fathers,
            the Pharaohs, were black.
Tell the white world;
let them know Hannibal
            was my brother.
And that the temples soothed in blackness
were the toys of a
foolish girl.

TRELLIE: I AM FULL OF HER

Lance Jeffers

I am full of her:
every blackness of her,
every Africanness,
every Georgia richness of her washes down my throat,
I swallow her beauty, it becomes the tissue of my intestines.

What have I done that she came by here, Lord, came by here?

What have I done to sign this spiritual with my scrawl,
    she standing at my shoulder,
the wondrous sign of love in her eye?

Five:
REBELS

GROWING CLEAN

Donald Green

When I was a kid
I used to get up
Every saturday
Morning and wash.
Sometimes for two
Or three hours.

When I came out
I'd look at my skin
And it was so clear
I'd go to mama and say:

"Look, I'm getting white."

She'd smile, agree
And go on with her chores.
Things have changed so
Much since then.

I hardly wash any more.

TELEGRAM TO ONE ROTTEN STEPMOTHER

Donald Green

Death comes to the eyes
Of those who are rotting
Inside.

America, when shall I send
You flowers?

POEM FOR A CERTAIN BLACK WOMAN

Donald Green

Black Woman, stop being whores for their world.
Stop letting them smoke you and tap your parts into ash trays.
The black men of the world are needing you.
And always kicking your feet on broadway stages ain't gittin' it.
Always turning your black hearts to cold diamond
Won't make the people better.

        It's been a long struggle
        And we still are strugglers
        Struggling to free ourselves
        From the dark place of their souls

        It gets so hard at times
        We curse you
        We get bitter you know
        We walk out and leave you cold

But we too are tired of matriarchs.
We too are tired of feeding hungry boys and girls into
An already unfree world.
At times we stoop low   but all is to come up
To pinch the stars and put the dust in our hearts.

        Let us not fight.
        You are the earth of me;
        Without you, there is no growing.

HARLEM FREEZE FRAME

Lebert Bethune

On the corner — 116th and Lenox
   all in brown down to his kickers,
     and leaning on a post like some gaudy warrior
     spear planted, patient eyes searching the veldt

This gleaming wrinkled blunthead old sweet-daddy
   smiles a grim smile
     as he hears a voice of Harlem scream
"WE ALL SUPPOSED TO BE DEAD BUT
WE AIN'T"
And his slow strut moves him on again.

IN MY JUGULAR

Lance Jeffers

Slaves stand on the block for sale in my jugular,
black and excremental from the ship;
the cane fields they will wade in choke my veins.
At the jugular's tip, the slave broker barks his call.
As long as I live, his insolence will sweep the burning coals
                    of outrage through my heart.

BLACK SOUL OF THE LAND

Lance Jeffers

I saw an old black man walk down the road,
a Georgia country road.
I stopped and asked where the nearest town might lie
where I could find a meal.
I might have driven on then to the town nearby
but I stayed to talk to the old black man
and read the future in his eyes.

His face was leathered, lean, and strong,
gashed with struggle scars.
His eyes were piercing, weary, red,
but in the old grief-soul that stared
through his eyes at me
and in the humble frame bent with humiliation and age,
there stood a secret manhood tough and tall
that circumstance and crackers could not kill:
a secret spine unbent within a spine,
a secret source of steel,
a secret sturdy rugged love,
a secret crouching hate,
a secret knife within his hand,
a secret bullet in his eye.

Give me your spine, old man, old man,
give me your rugged hate,
give me your sturdy oak-tree love,
give me your source of steel:
Teach me to sing so that the song may be mine
"Keep your hands on the plow: hold on!"
One day the nation's soul shall turn black like yours
and America shall cease to be its name.

BREATH IN MY NOSTRILS

Lance Jeffers

Breath in my nostrils this breasty spring day
shouts a jubilee
like one of my old sweaty fathers
in the surge of song and
sweetness of green trees and
the steamy blacky earth,
he lifted his head to a wildhorse tilt
And forgot that he was a slave!

THE WHITE HOUSE

Claude McKay

Your door is shut against my tightened face,
And I am sharp as steel with discontent;
But I possess the courage and the grace
To bear my anger proudly and unbent.
The pavement slabs burn loose beneath my feet,
A chafing savage, down the decent street,
And passion rends my vitals as I pass,
Where boldly shines your shuttered door of glass.
Oh I must search for wisdom every hour,
Deep in my wrathful bosom sore and raw,
And find in it the superhuman power
To hold me to the letter of your law!
Oh I must keep my heart inviolate
Against the potent poison of your hate.

IT WAS A FUNKY DEAL

Etheridge Knight

It was a funky deal.
The only thing real was red,
Red blood around his red, red beard.

It was a funky deal.

In the beginning was the word,
And in the end the deed.
Judas did it to Jesus
For the same Herd. Same reason.
You made them mad, Malcolm. Same reason.

It was a funky deal.

You rocked too many boats, man.
Pulled too many coats, man.
Saw through the jive.
You reached the wild guys
Like me. You and Bird. (And that
Lil Leroi cat.)

It was a funky deal.

HE SEES THROUGH STONE

Etheridge Knight

He sees through stone
he has the secret
eyes this old black one
who sits under prison skies
sits pressed by the sun
against the western wall
his pipe between purple gums

the years fall
like over-ripe plums
bursting red flesh
on the dark earth

his time is not my time
but I have known him
in a time now gone

he led me trembling cold
into the dark forest
taught me the secret rites
to take a woman
to be true to my brothers
to make my spear drink
the blood
of my enemies.

now black cats circle him
flash white teeth
snarl at the air
mashing green grass beneath
shining muscles
ears peeling his words
he smiles
he knows

the hunt   the enemy
he has the secret eyes
he sees through stone

TREE OF HEAVEN
(Ailanthus Altissima)

Naomi Long Madgett

I will live.
The ax's angry edge against my trunk
Cannot deny me. Though I thunder down
To lie prostrate among exalted grasses
That do not mourn me,
I will rise.

I will grow:
Persistent roots deep-burrowed in the earth
Avenge my fall. Tentacles will shoot out swiftly
In all directions, stubborn leaves explode their force
Into the sun.
I will thrive.

Curse of the orchard,
Blemish on the land's fair countenance,
I have grown strong for strength denied, for struggle
In hostile woods. I keep alive by being the troublesome,
Indestructible
Stinkweed of truth.

UNCLE JIM

Countee Cullen

"White folks is white," says uncle Jim;
"A platitude," I sneer;
And then I tell him so is milk,
And the froth upon his beer.

His heart walled up with bitterness,
He smokes his pungent pipe,
And nods at me as if to say,
"Young fool, you'll soon be ripe!"

I have a friend who eats his heart
Away with grief of mine,
Who drinks my joy as tipplers drain
Deep goblets filled with wine.

I wonder why here at his side,
Face-in-the-grass with him,
My mind should stray the Grecian urn
To muse on uncle Jim.

THE REBEL

Mari Evans

When I
die
I'm sure
I will have a
Big Funeral . . .
Curiosity
seekers . . .
coming to see
if I
am really
Dead . . .
or just
trying to make
Trouble . . .

WEAPONED WOMAN

Gwendolyn Brooks

Well, life has been a baffled vehicle
And baffling. But she fights, and
Has fought, according to her lights and
The lenience of her whirling place.

She fights with semi-folded arms,
Her strong bag, and the stiff
Frost of her face (that challenges "When" and "If.")
And altogether she does Rather Well.

Six:
BLACK LAMPS

BLACK MOTHER PRAYING

Owen Dodson

My great God, You been a tenderness to me,
Through the thick and through the thin;
You been a pilla to my soul;
You been like the shinin light a mornin in the black dark,
A elevator to my spirit.

Now there's a fire in this land like a last judgment,
And I done sat down by the rivers of Babylon
And wept deep when I remembered Zion,
Seein the water that can't quench fire
And the fire that burn up rivers.
Lord, I'm gonna say my say real quick and simple:

You know bout this war that's bitin the skies and gougin out the
                earth.
Last month, Lord, I bid my last boy away to fight.
I got all my boys fightin now for they country.
Didn't think bout it cept it were for freedom;
Didn't think cause they was black they wasn't American;
Didn't think a thing cept that they was my only sons,
And there was mothers all over the world
Sacrificin they sons like You let Yours be nailed
To the wood for men to behold the right.

Now I'm a black mother, Lord, I knows that now,
Black and burnin in these burnin times.
I can't hold my peace cause peace ain't fit to mention
When they's fightin right here in our streets
Like dogs — mongrel dogs and hill cats.
White is fightin black right here where hate abides like a cancer
                                  wound
And Freedom is writ big and crossed out:
Where, bless God, they's draggin us outta cars
In Texas and California, in Newark, Detroit,

Blood on the darkness, Lord, blood on the pavement,
Leaviñ us moanin and afraid.
What has we done?
Where and when has we done?
They's plantin the seeds of hate down in our bone marrow
When we don't want to hate.

We don't speak much in the street where I live, my God,
Nobody speak much, but we thinkin deep
Of the black sons in lands far as the wind can go,
Black boys fightin this war with them.

We thinkin deep bout they sisters stitchin airplane canvas,
And they old fathers plowin for wheat,
And they mothers bendin over washtubs,
They brothers at the factory wheels:
They all is bein body beat and spirit beat and heart sore and
                            wonderin.

Listen, Lord, they ain't nowhere for black mothers to turn.
Won't You plant Your Son's goodness in this land
Before it too late?
Set Your stars of sweetness twinklin over us like winda lamps
Before it too late?
Help these men to see they losin while they winnin
Long as they allow theyselves to lynch in the city streets and
                      on country roads?

When can I pray again,
View peace in my own parlor again?
When my sons come home
How can I show em my broken hands?

How can I show em they sister's twisted back?
How can I present they land to them?
How, when they been battlin in far places for freedom?
Better let em die in the desert drinkin sand
Or holdin onto water and shippin into death
Than they come back an see they sufferin for vain.

I done seen a man runnin for his life,
Runnin like the wind from a mob, to no shelter.
Where were a hidin place for him?
Saw a dark girl nine years old
Cryin cause her father done had
The light scratched from his eyes in the month of June.

Where the seein place for him?
A black boy lyin with his arms huggin the pavement in pain.
What he starin at?
Good people hands up, searched for guns and razors and pipes.
When they gonna pray again?

How, precious God, can I watch my son's eyes
When they hear this terrible?
How can I pray again when my tongue
Is near cleavin to the roof of my mouth?
Tell me, Lord, how?

Every time they strike us, they strikin Your Son;
Every time they shove us in, they cornerin they own children.
I'm gonna scream before I hope again.
I ain't never gonna hush my mouth or lay down this heavy, black,
                           weary, terrible load
Until I fights to stamp my feet with my black sons
On a freedom solid rock and stand there peaceful
And look out into the star wilderness of the sky
And the land lyin about clean, and secure land,
And people not afraid again.

Lord, let us all see the golden wheat together,
Harvest the harvest together,
Touch the fulness and the hallelujah together.
                                     Amen.

PASSIVE RESISTANCE

Margaret Danner

And to this Man who turned the other cheek,
this Man who murmured not a word,
or fought at persecutors,
remained meek under it all,
I crawl, in wonder.

For as the evil tongues begin to turn on me
I want to fight, strike back,
and see them quail
in some rat-ridden jail,
or suffering for
the suffering they've caused.
I want no more of this humility.
But I must bow,
bow low before it now,
and love the evil ones,
as You did. Yet, I am sure
it was much easier for
God's son.

CHILD IN THE NIGHT

May Miller

I heard a child cry in the night
And saw light fill a window
Across the areaway.

Half in sleep I saw and heard,
For I was the mother bringing light,
I was the baby born of me.

I was the omniscient night
Curved to a world of need
As a pulsing instrument.

I am the edge of morning
Waking keen to myself
On a single pillow touching nothing.

THREE SCENES FOR ALL MEN

May Miller

He knows Gethsemane;
Driven to its solitude,
Has sharpened to his need
Its awful silences.

And Golgotha —
The jeers, the colored cloak,
The long and weary way
To a storm-dark hill.

He knows the Third Day —
The faith that all unnoticed
Stayed a while
To hear him from the tomb.

HUMBLED ROCKS

Paulette Childress White

When I was little
I thought them funny —
those old Sisters
bending their bodies
like stunted shadows
before candle-lit altars,
grotesque faces like
ceremonial masks
that seethed prayer
and shouted glory
through gaping mouths.
It seemed to me
even that Perfect God
they prayed to
(if He looked on them at all)
must have thought them crude
abstractions of His image
and closed His ear
to their coarse supplications.

Now
growing through modifications
of their pain —
learning our fierce legacy,
I do not think them funny.
Now
I lean on them
needing sometimes
to ground myself in their faith.
They are souls turned out for me
lighting the way we've come
the way we go on.
They are not stunted shadows
but the humbled rocks
I build on.
Surely God
must look upon them well
and hear.

BIG MAYBELLE

Paulette Childress White

I've heard them all singing
felt the magic of their voices
pouring into empty air
I have been lifted up
to the glorious clouds
bursting like fat fruit
with the joy they give

I've heard them all singing
been beat so bad with blues
that my soul crunched
and rolled like a dead weed
at their feet

I have been in touch
with some mighty souls singing
but

Big Maybelle blew out a song
so strong she moved me
away

Beyond words
it is her voice going down
in me, telling me
the Ancient Mother lives,
telling me who
I am

Big Maybelle blew out
a song so strong she moved me
                                      away

OBITUARY

Robert Hayden

My father's hands
Were gnarled and hard,
The fruits of their labor
He shared with the Lord.
His roots sat deep
In the rock of the Word,
In Abraham's bosom
He nestled like a bird.
When I was a child,
I sat at his knee,
He opened The Book
And read to me
Of Salome dancing
Columnar and faulty
And Lot's wife standing
Forlorn and salty;
Of Salome dancing
For the head of the evangel
And Jacob wresting
Blessings from an angel.
Cymbals and roses
And bronze and myrrh,
Flame and thunder
Those stories were . . . .
And closing The Book
With gaze stern and level
My father would counsel,
"My son, shun evil."
Though life was marshes
And dark journeyings,
He lived as one
Prepared for wings.
He died quietly
One sun-white morn,
Just as spring was
Being born.
He died serenely,
Having found
God's footprints flowering
On mortal ground.

BUT I SAY

Jill Witherspoon Boyer

life's not about the valiant stride
of love they say
not about the sun brightening
in our hands
or in rivers running yes
and they say
that we can grow
amid the unloved ugly little pieces
that set our grinding teeth
against the boiling need
and if we lose
an arm a leg
in lonely battles
then what was wholeness anyway
but I say
season into season
is how we'll grow
and toward a caring place
I know is there
where we can watch the golden overflow
being smiled on small brown faces
that look like us

DANNY TAKES THE BUS

Naomi Faust

We knew well
the morning sun
had not warmed the earth
as he arose,
sleep still tugging at his face.
He had to hustle
or he would be late.
He had to catch the mustard yellow bus.

We knew well
he could not unarm himself
of the wonderment of his new school:
the seats glossed with varnish,
the floors licking clean,
the corridors light and cheery
and dressed in such appetizers
as beckon each passerby
to bite into their being.

But at lunch he was as alone
as a single little tree in a barren valley.
He wedged quietly into a far-away seat
and shrank gently into a ball
as the smell of fresh food
curled up beside his nose.
He listened to the fledglings' voices.
He watched swarms of white bodies,
their movements lithe
as they swayed to
the rise of the youthful din.

We knew, too,
that for Danny
a first year in a top starred school
had not been easy.
In his class,
high-key perception
flew all about him,
and teaching swelled to full-based range.

Studies at his new place
had been difficult for him.
He had not been nurtured in fertile soil.
And as the battle of wits
surrounded him,
memories of his neighborhood school
almost drowned his thoughts:
the battered seats, the gloomy walls,
the feeble books, the miser labs.

We knew well
he'd not turn back his chance.
Perhaps another year's harvest
would bring more fruitful gains.
Perhaps Tom and Jake and Larry
would join him.
They'd bring softness to his load.
We knew well
he would not give in.

FOR BILLY AND HELEN'S SECOND

Houston A. Baker, Jr.

People will stop
and listen to your words
salute your wisdom

Soft winds will carry you
in their journeyings

And among your own dark nations
they will call

      Sister Schaan, Sister Schaan

          Strong and Lovely

Sister Schaan.

AUTHOR INDEX

Alexander, Lewis, 39

Baker, Houston A., Jr., 57, 70, 104
Bennett, Gwendolyn B., 61
Bethune, Lebert, 78
Boyer, Jill Witherspoon, 101
Brooks, Gwendolyn, 88
Brooks, Jonathan Henderson, 51
Brown, Sterling A., 23, 24, 52

Clifton, Lucille, 16
Cullen, Countee, 86

Danner, Margaret, 95
Davis, Gloria, 71
Derricotte, Toi, 42
Dodson, Owen, 36-37, 91-94

Emanuel, James A., 41
Evans, Mari, 47, 87

Faust, Naomi, 102-103

Govan, Donald D., 17
Green, Donald, 75, 76, 77
Grimké, Angelina Weld, 29

Hayden, Robert, 40, 55, 100
Hughes, Langston, 30, 64, 65

Jeffers, Lance, 38, 56, 72, 79, 80, 81
Johnson, Georgia Douglas, 22, 45, 46
Johnson, James Weldon, 26

Knight, Etheridge, 66, 83, 84

Lee, Don L. (See Madhubuti, Haki)
Lomax, Pearl Cleage, 25, 58
Lorde, Audre, 19, 63

Madgett, Naomi Long, 35, 53, 54, 67, 85
Madhubuti, Haki (Don L. Lee), 19, 62
McKay, Claude, 34, 82
Miller, May, 33, 96, 97

Okara, Gabriel, 48-49

Randall, Dudley, 50, 69

Spriggs, Edward S., 18

Toomer, Jean, 31, 32

White, Paulette Childress, 15, 68, 98, 99